A 30-DAY DEVOTIONAL FOR SENIORS

SENIOR

PREPARING FOR THE FUTURE

LARS ROOD

simply for students

YouthMinistry.com/TOGETHER

Senior
Preparing for the Future

© 2013 Lars Rood / 0000 0001 2378 3544

group.com
simplyyouthministry.com

Credits
Author: Lars Rood
Executive Developer: Nadim Najm
Chief Creative Officer: Joani Schultz
Editor: Rob Cunningham
Cover Art and Production: Veronica Preston

ISBN   978-0-7644-9005-7

10 9 8 7   20 19 18 17 16

Printed in the U.S.A.

TO SOREN:

The year you are a senior is going to be a tough one for me. I love watching you grow and make decisions, and I'll be honest and say that when you leave to a new thing, it'll be really hard. But I'm already so proud of you and know that God is growing you and will use you for great things.

CONTENTS

INTRODUCTION

The senior year can feel a little bit bizarre. I see it broken up into three distinct parts. At the beginning of the year, you are excited to finally be a senior and have all the privileges and prestige of being the oldest kids on campus. But at the same time, you are scrambling to figure out where you'll apply to college and getting those crazy applications and essays completed. Or maybe you're thinking about a different path: the military, or a job, or vocational training, or a family business. Whatever your plans for life after high school, this can be a pretty stressful season of life.

But then things slow down considerably. You've reached the middle of the year, and there isn't as much to do. If you're going to college, you might be waiting for envelopes in the mail that will reveal your options for next year, but in general this period of time is a little more relaxing. Then near the end of your senior year, it ramps up again as you get ready to graduate and prepare to pursue your future plans—while also saying goodbye to so much of your past.

In all of this, your faith journey can get off track or take a little bit of a beating if you don't stay focused on the things that are most important. It's easy to get distracted and to feel like your faith doesn't matter as much anymore because you are getting ready to leave so much of your life behind. During this time, though, it is particularly important to lean into your youth group, church, Christian friends, leaders, family members, and your Bible because even if you've built a firm foundation, you need to keep building on it before you enter a world where everything is different.

How this book works:

This devotional includes 30 short things for you to think about. For each reading you'll find some sort of story and some follow-up questions to consider. You can do these by yourself, but you also can benefit from discussing them with a small group of people. This book might become 30 weeks of curriculum or simply provide 30 days of focus before the school year starts.

Each devotion includes a section called "The World Thinks." Most often these are comments that I have heard from non-Christians about these particular topics or issues. I don't hold back, so they may come across as a little negative. That's OK. You'll hear negative things all the time about your faith. The point is to encourage you to think through what people say and work out how you might respond to the thoughts and reactions people have about your faith in Christ.

You'll also find an action step for each devotion that is exactly what it sounds like: an opportunity to actually do something to discover and apply key truths. Often these are things that take some effort to accomplish and can help you grow. I want to encourage you to really put effort into doing them. Finally, I've included some Bible passages for you to look up—often several, but sometimes just one or two. I want you to go deeper and explore other places in the Bible with more thoughts, stories, truths, and ideas that will help you.

It's my hope and prayer that these devotions will challenge you, encourage you, and put you in places where you will have the opportunity to prepare for the future.

SECTION 1

THE BUSY SEASON

Hooray, you're a senior—now figure out what to do with the rest of your life! Fill out all these applications and essays, and get it done as soon as possible so you can register early and get everything figured out quickly! At the same time, get ready for your "last" everything in high school and be excited that your future life is coming so quickly!

The beginning of your senior year can be really fun and really stressful at the same time. You may need to make one last push to get your grades up to get into that school you want, or you might be padding your resume with a few more volunteer opportunities so you can look well rounded. Or maybe you're not even sure you want to go to college and you're struggling to find people to talk with who won't push you to go that way simply because it's "normal."

Emotions and stress run high during this part of the year, and you need to focus on your faith and on today's realities, and allow the future to come slowly without trying to make it happen sooner than it needs to. God has an awesome plan for you, but a lot of other people also want to offer input and suggestions—and you are finally at a place where you are going to be making choices, which can be incredible and scary.

№.1 WILL THIS YEAR BE GREAT?

Your senior year should be great. And it likely will be. You're at the top of the school and are finally a big man (or woman) on campus—for nine months, at least. And then it's over. But while it lasts, it will be amazing.

I remember the first month of my senior year—everything changed. The cliques that had been around for years seemed to disappear in my senior class. All of a sudden, everyone was much more open and accepting of each other. Honestly, it was a little bit weird, but it got me thinking that this was what the next phase of life would be like! I remember thinking that in college there wouldn't be all the weirdness and insular groups of people—and that if anything felt weird like that, I'd just walk away and find new people to hang out with.

There is so much to look forward to this senior year, so enjoy every bit of it. Keep a journal. Take lots of photos. Do whatever it takes to remember all these incredible moments.

THINK ABOUT:

1. What are you most looking forward to your senior year? Why?

2. Is there anything you are particularly nervous or worried about? If so, why?

3. How do you think your relationship with God needs to grow or change this year?

THE WORLD THINKS:

You are finally at the top. Take every opportunity to remind everyone younger than you how important you are. After all, that's what the seniors did to you, right?

ACT:

As you think about this school year, consider some specific things that you might want to accomplish. Get a piece of paper and write down several of those things and share them with two friends. See what they're looking forward to accomplishing, too.

READ:

Ezekiel 38:23, Luke 9:43, and Philippians 3:8

No. 2 WHO ARE YOU SUPPOSED TO BE?

Like a lot of people, I wasn't fully prepared for my senior year. I'd become comfortable not being in charge and having people to look up to at school. For me it was a little different, too, because my older sister was just one grade ahead of me and I was close to many of her friends. So when they all left, I faced a void that I wasn't really ready for. Deciding how to fill that void and figuring out who I was supposed to be—it all was a little bit tricky.

I had a distinct place at school, though, because I was in band and was actually pretty good at my instrument. So my senior year that was my go-to place for feeling comfortable and having a lot of encouragement and praise come my way. I was pretty sure that I would be doing something with music in college, too, so it didn't feel like I was going to lose that part of my identity. I can imagine, though, that if you are an athlete who isn't planning on playing any sports at the college level, your senior year might be tougher as you realize you are going to be leaving that behind. Trying to figure out who you are supposed to be your senior year isn't always tough for everyone, but it does have pieces that can be difficult to walk through.

What about your identity? Has it been defined by a sport, an extracurricular activity, or a group of friends? Remember that who you are is so much deeper than what you do. Your value and purpose surpass any activity, club, social group, or job— not just now, but for the rest of your life!

THINK ABOUT:

1. What are some of the roles you think or know you will have as a senior?

2. How can you figure out who you are supposed to be this year?

3. What role do you think your faith can play as you figure out your identity as a senior and how to handle the changes at the end of the year?

THE WORLD THINKS:

Your options are limited once you graduate from high school. Everyone has something that they are specifically suited for, and you have to figure that out. Trying to be something different or unique or innovative will just cause you to fail.

ACT:

Think about one thing you wish you had done in high school that you've never tried—a sport, a leadership role, an extracurricular activity, or maybe some kind of community involvement. Is now the right time to see if that is something you could do? Ask some people you trust to help push you to try something new.

READ:

Joshua 1:9, Psalm 13:5-6, and Proverbs 3:5-6

№.3 WHAT DO YOU WANT TO DO?

I recently told a friend that years ago I really wanted to be either a tow truck driver or a taxi cab driver. I had a lot of gifts that would have made me good at either of those careers. I memorize streets well, like working hard, can talk to people I don't know, and enjoy working alone and being my own boss. Sometimes I wish I hadn't walked away from those jobs because every now and then they sound more inviting than what I'm doing. But I know that neither of those jobs was what God had called me to do.

In college I started out studying computer science, then politics, then English, and finally became a teacher. God made it pretty clear to me through a series of people and opportunities that he had designed me to work with students.

You may not have a clue what you want to do with your life right now—and that's OK. If I had locked myself into a career path too early, I would have missed out on a life of ministry. But it's OK to have some dreams and ideas; just hold them loosely because God may totally change your plans. He did with mine.

THINK ABOUT:

1. If you had to choose right now, what career path would you follow? Why?

2. What are some things you really like but don't feel you could do as a career?

3. What gifts and talents do you think God has given you that maybe you haven't fully figured out how to implement yet?

THE WORLD THINKS:

Whatever you do make sure it pays and pays well. You'll have bills to pay, a home to maintain, and a family to support. Who cares if you don't really enjoy your job or find it fulfilling? Get your head out of the clouds and face reality.

ACT:

Because you will probably have some free space and not be too busy this year, see if you can find some people in careers that you might want to pursue and ask if you can shadow them for a few hours at work. Ask lots of questions: how they prepared for the career, what they enjoy most (and least), how they make a difference through their job, and what other advice they might offer.

READ:

Psalm 20:4, Proverbs 15:22, Proverbs 16:9, and Ephesians 1:11

ꜰᴏ.4 WHO CAN YOU TURN TO?

I didn't really have a very good support system of people I could turn to my senior year. My parents were always there and loved and cared for me, and they were certainly a big part of my decision-making process. But I never really shared my heart and my hopes with them. My youth group had fallen apart just before my senior year when my youth pastor and his wife separated and the church didn't hire anyone to replace him. My friends were in a similar place as me—trying to figure out a lot on their own.

My older sister was a big help for me as I tried to navigate my senior year and decide what I wanted to do after graduation. Because she graduated just a year before me, I saw a lot of her journey. She ended up going to college only about an hour away, so I went and visited her often because I liked her—and because I needed help with my math homework.

It's important to have people around you who will support you, encourage you, help you process your questions, listen to your dreams, and pray for God's direction and strength in your life. Maybe your parents or siblings can fill that role. Maybe your friends or classmates or people at church can. Seek out these kinds of people in your life—and if you can't easily find them, pray that God will lead you to them!

THINK ABOUT:

1. Who are some people you believe you can turn to for help, wisdom, or insight?

2. If you don't have those people in your life, how can you make wise decisions?

3. What are some tough decisions you've had to make, and how has it been helpful to have others walk alongside you?

4. Where does God fit in all this for you?

THE WORLD THINKS:

Ultimately you are going to have to make the decisions that feel the most right to you, so just do what you think you should. Besides, everyone has their own opinion, so if you ask lots of people, you'll get lots of different, confusing, contradictory advice. Who needs that?

ACT:

It's time to practice. You likely are thinking about some things that you don't know how to handle, or some decisions you don't know if you can make wisely. Write out a couple of those things; find an adult or friend you trust, and ask for advice.

READ:

Deuteronomy 30:10, Isaiah 45:22, Daniel 9:3, and Acts 14:15

№.5 HOW DO YOU CHOOSE?

I ended up getting into almost every college I applied to—both a good and a bad thing. It would have been nice if God had helped a little more by narrowing down my options, but he didn't. I had to choose among six different schools. It was funny at the time because I felt like I had so many possibilities and options ahead of me, but I struggled to make the decision.

Ultimately I decided to go to the same Christian college that my sister attended. One reason I made this choice was because I had spent a lot of time visiting her and hearing about how much she liked it, and it just started to grow on me. Another factor was hearing that several friends from my youth group had all decided to go there as well. Those things certainly helped, but it still was a tough decision.

Financially it would have been so much better to go somewhere else because that school was really expensive. It put a major burden on my parents, and I also ended up with a lot of student loans. But it was the right place for me. I can say now with absolutely no doubt that God wanted me at that school and that he used it to pave the way for me to be in ministry today.

Your post-graduation path may appear clear and obvious, but if you're facing lots of options—or seemingly no options at all—trust in God's ability to lead and guide you. Pray for God's wisdom, and seek input from trusted people in your life. Following God's plan may require a step of faith, but he certainly will bless you for taking that step!

THINK ABOUT:

1. When you've had to make hard decisions, what have you done? How have you made your decisions?

2. Have you ever made a tough decision that you now believe was wrong? What process did you use to make that decision, and what did you learn from the experience that might help you next time you're in a similar situation?

3. How will you ultimately decide what you will do next year?

4. Where do you believe God is in all of this?

THE WORLD THINKS:

Don't stress; there isn't just one place you should go or just one thing you should do. Choose what feels right and go for it.

ACT:

Find an adult (or a couple of them) and ask them how they made these kinds of decisions. Hear their stories and ask how they feel now about the decisions they made then.

READ:

Psalm 37:4, Psalm 119:30-32, Ephesians 1:11, and
Colossians 3:12

NO.6 HOW ARE YOU HANDLING OTHER PEOPLE'S EXPECTATIONS?

I think Jesus did a pretty good job of managing expectations. A lot of people expected him to be something different from what he was, but he just didn't really address their issue—he simply went about doing what he was called to do. You may be in a situation where everyone else seems to have a plan for your life, and you have to figure out how to reconcile that with your own plans and with your understanding of God's plans.

Let's start with your parents. They may have high expectations that you would go to a particular school and have a specific career so that you will make enough money and they won't have to take care of you. But what if you want to be a missionary or take a gap year before college or attend a trade school or enter the military? Those would be very different plans from what your parents would like you to do. How do you negotiate through all of that with them? This is an important skill, but I'm confident that can work through it (even if just slowly and patiently) and figure it out.

THINK ABOUT:

1. What plans do you think your parents have for you? How have they communicated their hopes and dreams and plans—or have they?

2. How do your parents' desires line up with what you want to do?

3. Where does God fit into your parents' plants or your plans?

THE WORLD THINKS:

You decide what to do—and if your parents don't like it, that's their problem.

ACT:

The best way of managing expectations is to communicate honestly and frequently. Avoid springing something on your parents or other important people that they didn't expect. But the responsibility rests on you to get this started. Pick a time with your parents or guardians to sit down and ask them what they expect. Then begin to share with them your heart and what you want and what you sense God revealing in your life.

READ:

Psalm 5:3, Psalm 62:5, Jeremiah 29:11, and Hebrews 4:12

№7 WHAT DOES IT MEAN TO HAVE A WHOLE YEAR OF LASTS?

In the *Freshman* devotional that's part of this series, I devoted an entire section to "A whole year of firsts"—and now a similar event is happening to you. You get to experience everything in high school for the very *last* time. For some of you, that's a good thing. You are glad this dance, that test, this concert, or that sport is over. You're just ready for it all to be done so you can get out of here. But some of you might really mourn when you experience endings. What if you have played a sport your whole life and know you aren't going to compete in college? The last game or practice will have a whole different meaning for you. Senior year can be a series of disappointments if you struggle to say goodbye to people and things.

At the same time, though, you have the opportunity to fully embrace these experiences because you know that they are ending. What if you went all out for that last homecoming experience and created amazing memories? You have the freedom to push yourself on the playing field without regrets because it's the final game. There is a side of doing things the last time that can really be freeing when you know that you are moving on to something new and different. Enjoy it, embrace it, celebrate it, and allow it to shape you.

THINK ABOUT:

1. What is something you are looking forward to ending? Why?

2. What things are you not looking forward to doing for the last time? Why?

3. How do you feel knowing that this is your last year to experience all of this?

4. Where do you think God is in all of this for you?

THE WORLD THINKS:

Just get over it and move on. You will likely not remember any of this in the future anyway. Life is full of endings, so get used to it.

ACT:

Your senior year is a great time to make memories—work on creating great ones. Think about something specific you could do with your friends that would be a lasting memory and would give back to the school or the community. Share your idea with some adults, and invite them to help you accomplish it.

READ:

Genesis 25:7-8, Psalm 45:6, Isaiah 51:6, and Revelation 22:13

№8 DO YOU HAVE APPLICATION ANTICIPATION?

Few things bring more stress to the senior year than college applications. Everyone pushes you to get them in on time, and you have to figure out how to do them well while still juggling all the other pieces of your life. And college essays tend to be even more stressful when you feel like you have to somehow share a story that will make an admissions counselor think you are a great candidate—even if your grades and test scores aren't as good as they should be. The frustrating thing is you may already know exactly where you want to go to school, but you have to fill out all these *other* applications just in case you don't get into your top choice. This can be a really discouraging and frustrating season.

One thing that also can be really hard is if you are solid in your faith and want God to direct your steps and your path, but you just don't feel like he's doing things in the timing you need. If God would just show up and tell you what to do, you know you'd listen—but he doesn't seem to be doing things on your schedule! So you fill out all these applications and hope to get back thick admissions packets to schools and not skinny rejection letters. Talk about a tough season where you need God.

THINK ABOUT:

1. What things are most worried about during this application season?

2. What will you do if you get into every school you apply to? How will you decide where to go?

3. If God made it clear what he wanted you to do, but it was not at all what you wanted, how would you decide which path to follow?

THE WORLD THINKS:

Don't stress; college doesn't really matter anyway. It's a lot of money for a piece of paper that you'll never look at again.

ACT:

If you really believe God is leading you and directing your path, take all your college applications and put them in a big pile and ask some of your Christian friends and even your parents to join you in a time praying over them. Ask God to let his path be known, and pray that you would be open and available to God's will. And even if you sense God leading you in a direction that has nothing to do with college, it's still a great idea to gather with trusted friends and family members to pray for God's guidance!

READ:

Proverbs 23:18, Ecclesiastes 8:7, and Romans 8:38-39

№9 WHAT IF YOU DON'T FEEL READY?

I'll be the first to admit I didn't feel ready for life after high school. I was really enjoying my senior year. All the changes and the freedoms made for a totally different experience compared to the three previous years. Plus, I hadn't had a lot of opportunity to make choices for myself, so when I started thinking about what I should do and where I should go, it was really scary. I had a strong faith but didn't know if it would be enough to help me with the temptation and struggles I'd face.

Plus, I was shy and worried about starting over after high school and concerned about how I would meet friends. The last time I'd moved had been really difficult, and I didn't want to do that again. Fortunately, God used all of my senior year to prepare me to leave, and it was OK that in the first few months I wasn't ready because by the end of the year I was raring to go.

How about your experience and your expectations? Do you feel prepared for what will happen next? Remember that you aren't taking these steps alone; God is with you, and your family and friends will lovingly support and encourage you in your next season of life.

THINK ABOUT:

1. What are some of your fears about leaving high school?

2. How do you think you can be better prepared for this big transition in your life?

3. Do you trust that God has brought you to this point and won't leave you unprepared? Why or why not?

THE WORLD THINKS:

No one is really prepared for life after high school. You just go for it and hope for the best. Things work out well for some people and not so well for others.

ACT:

You'll likely need to learn some things before you enter your post-graduation season of life. That list could include simple things such as how to do laundry—or difficult things such as knowing how to fully resist temptation. Make a list of some of these things and find an adult in your church or leader in your youth group and ask them to help you get prepared. (Your parents can probably help with the laundry part!)

READ:

Psalm 23, Psalm 85:13, Isaiah 40:3, and Ephesians 2:10

№10 DOES GOD REALLY HAVE A PLAN FOR YOUR LIFE?

My senior year of high school, I think I probably would have answered that question with a no. It wasn't that I didn't believe that God had plans; I just wasn't sure God was going to tell me mine. I thought I was going to have to figure it out on my own because God didn't seem to be revealing it to me in the timing I felt was appropriate. Often we spend so much time thinking about the plans we have for our own lives that we box God in and tell him we are happy to hear his plans as long as they fit in the categories we've created.

I have a close friend who's been a missionary for YWAM (Youth With a Mission) for almost 20 years. He felt called into missions early in his life, and ever since then he has been following God's leading. And those plans have changed a lot. He has filled a bunch of different roles and jobs within the mission field but still believes he is exactly where God wants him to be—even when God uses him in different or unexpected ways. You may be struggling to understand or recognize the exact details of God's plan, but perhaps right now his plan is just that you would stay close to him and continue to listen to him as he shapes, molds, and prepares you.

THINK ABOUT:

1. Are you OK with not fully knowing God's plan for your life? Why or why not?

2. What are some things you feel like God is directing you toward, and why?

3. How will you make decisions if you don't know God's plan for you?

THE WORLD THINKS:

You will likely have multiple jobs and careers and directions in your life. Just pick the one right now that feels the most right and do it.

ACT:

In your small group or youth group, pick a project that you want to do that will help people. If you have a shelter or soup kitchen nearby, volunteer to help out. Even when you don't have things figured out for your future, you can be used in your present to help those in need.

READ:

Isaiah 30:1, Jeremiah 29:11, Ezekiel 37, and Hebrews 11:40

SECTION 2

SLOW AND LOW

There will come a point in your senior year where things just slow down; you'll look around and try to figure out what you are supposed to do. The fall semester is almost over and you are just waiting—waiting to hear back from colleges where you've applied, or from the military recruiters, or from the vocational training program. This can be a really fun season because you probably have less to do and can just enjoy what it means to be a senior. This can be a fun time that you fully experience while it lasts.

But even in this season, you can be reflecting on, praying about, and figuring out some important things. If you're involved in a small group or youth group, this is a great time to lean into the conversations and see if a leader can talk about making choices and preparing you for handling difficult decisions about the next stage of your life. This is also probably a good season to learn (or improve) some important skills from your parents such as doing laundry, managing a budget, and making choices about what to eat. You will benefit from growing in those types of skills and habits before you graduate.

NO. 11 HAVING PATIENCE

I've never been a patient person. I hate to wait. I get myself in more trouble over timing and impatience than anything else in my life. And this isn't a new struggle; it's sort of always been this way.

Some of you are like me. You struggle with waiting on answers. But it's a skill set that we need to learn. I can't tell you the number of times in my life when I haven't wanted to be patient and wait so I just made a decision—and it ended up being wrong.

My big weakness? Directions for a project. I hate taking the time to read through the directions for anything! I just want to put something together! I've found over the years, though, that pairing up with someone who has more patience than me is a good thing because that person can help me slow down and figure out what to do—instead of just jumping in and doing it. If you also struggle with patience, this may be a wise strategy to consider.

THINK ABOUT:

1. How patient of a person are you? What makes you impatient?

2. Sometimes God wants us to wait and the answer might be "not yet." How do you handle those moments, and how do you typically respond?

3. What are some tools and tricks you've learned that can help you when you are being impatient?

THE WORLD THINKS:

Patience is an obsolete idea. Who has time to wait in our fast-moving, ever-changing culture? We all deserve answers now, and we shouldn't ever have to be patient.

ACT:

Being patient is tough. We all want information and direction—and we want it now. But patience doesn't simply mean sitting around and doing nothing. There is no reason why you can't be actively doing something while you wait. What is something you've wanted to try for a long time but you have never pursued or attempted? Now is the time to figure out how to make it happen.

READ:

Proverbs 19:11, Galatians 5:22-23, Colossians 3:12, and Hebrews 6:12

NO. 12 LOOKING TO GOD

I'm really good at looking for answers, but sometimes I find myself Googling things before asking God for help and direction. As a pastor I'm embarrassed to admit that, but it can often be true. I know that if I type what I need into a search engine, I will get immediate results, but if I pray or look for answers in my Bible, it seems like I won't always find what I'm looking for. I hate admitting this because I'm trying to get you to be better than me.

Fortunately, I've learned a few tips that can help you. God speaks to me often through other people who are walking closely with him, too. So ask others what they think and look to them for advice. Often people have already gone through some of the things you're struggling with, so their stories can be a huge source of help. You also may benefit from Bible study tools—including programs on your computer—because you can use it like you use a search engine and often find a relevant passage of Scripture quickly.

THINK ABOUT:

1. What is the best way you've found for you to turn and listen to God?

2. What people in your life can speak God's truth to you?

3. How often do you read your Bible and look for answers?

THE WORLD THINKS:

Even if God really does exist, he certainly doesn't speak anymore, and the Bible was written thousands of years ago so that can't be a big help for you.

ACT:

Find a Bible concordance and look through it. Search for different words and phrases related to the issues that you often struggle with the most. Write out some verses and put them on your bathroom mirror.

READ:

Psalm 13:3, Psalm 39:7, Jonah 2:1-4, and John 17:1

№.13 DEALING WITH DISAPPOINTMENT

My car died my senior year of high school. It was an old Volkswagen® Bug that had clearly seen better days. I was anticipating getting a new car, but I didn't have any money and my parents would have to help out in a big way. My dad found what he thought would be the perfect car for me, but when I saw it—well, let's just say that I was a little underwhelmed. *Disappointed* is probably too strong of a word because at that point, any car was better than what I had—which was no car at all—but it certainly wasn't at all what I was hoping for. I don't really know what kind of car I wanted, but I know it wasn't the four-door hatchback VW Rabbit that I received.

I've had a few other major disappointments in life that have generally revolved around people. I had expectations that weren't met, and friends and family let me down. I think I have learned to handle things well, give grace to people, and have my hopes at the right levels, but it's still hard when something doesn't go the way you had planned.

You've likely encountered some disappointments from people or from situations that didn't unfold the way you had hoped. I wish I could tell you that you'll never encounter another disappointment in your life, but that wouldn't be the truth. We are imperfect humans interacting with imperfect humans, so disappointments will happen. Turn to trusted friends for comfort and a listening ear, and turn to God for strength and hope.

THINK ABOUT:

1. What disappointments have you already experienced? How did you handle them?

2. What is your go-to response when something doesn't go your way?

3. How do you think God has used or can use these disappointments and frustrations in your life?

THE WORLD THINKS:

Life is full of disappointments. You need to learn to get over it and move on.

ACT:

Now is a good time to think about what you will do if your future plans don't work out as you have planned. Who can you turn to when you face these disappointments? Talk to them now and come up with a plan of how they can help you if things don't go as hoped.

READ:

Deuteronomy 4:30-31, 2 Chronicles 15:4, Psalm 31:9, and Psalm 55:17

№.14 HANDLING OTHER PEOPLE'S EXPECTATIONS

I probably set myself up for this one. I was in band for years, all the way from sixth grade until my first few years of college. It was a large part of my identity and also the way my parents felt connected to something that I liked doing. And then I quit.

I think it was harder on my parents than on anyone else, including me. They loved coming to concerts, seeing me play at games, and watching me do solos and perform at different events. I won every major music award at my high school and received quite a few music scholarships to continue playing in college. But I just didn't want to do it anymore. I was burned out. I wish that I had taken the time to sit and talk to my parents about why I was quitting, but I didn't. I just announced one day that I was done—and that was it.

A lot of people have a lot of expectations about your senior year—expectations about where you will go to school, how much you are going to have to pay, whether or not you'll go into the military, what kind of job you might be able to find, and more. Working to help manage other people's expectations is a big and important skill that usually can be worked through by communicating consistently and effectively.

THINK ABOUT:

1. What expectations do you believe your parents or guardians have about your life after high school? Do your plans line up with what they want?

2. How can you best manage the expectations that others have of you?

3. What expectations do you think God has of you? How does thinking about that make you feel?

THE WORLD THINKS:

Everyone wants something from you. You will have to figure out how to do your own thing and not care what others think. Otherwise your life will always be centered on other people and their expectations, and not what you want or need.

ACT:

Ask your parents about their expectations for you. Listen to them and see why they have those hopes and goals for you. Talk about your own hopes and expectations, and see where they line up. Communicating these things is hugely important.

READ:

Job 17:15-16, Job 22:28, Psalm 5:3, Micah 6:8, and
Ephesians 6:1-4

№.15 FINDING MENTORS

I had a boss once who was a great mentor in my life—and he's still a great mentor to me. John hired me to work at a summer camp when I was in college and played a significant role in how I developed as a man. It took a while, though, before I was able to fully appreciate who he was and what he had to offer.

I hadn't ever really had that kind of experience growing up, and having someone speak truth with wisdom in my life was new to me. John had the ability to look at things from a very different perspective from me, and because he knew me well and cared for me, he was able to package his wisdom in a way that was perfect for me to hear.

It's similar to the idea that your parents could tell you the same thing over and over again, but when someone else packages the same truth in a slightly different way, you're finally ready to hear it. I realize that's not very fair to parents, and it is possible to have that kind of relationship with your parents. But the reality is that sometimes you need other people. My advice is to look for many trustworthy mentors and wise people who can speak truth to you.

THINK ABOUT:

1. What people have you gone to for answers in the past? How have they helped you?

2. What are some issues that you need someone to walk through with you?

3. What people has God put in your life already that might be key mentors and sources of wisdom for you?

THE WORLD THINKS:

Don't trust people because everyone has a hidden agenda. One of these days, you'll get burned.

ACT:

If you already have mentors in your life, go and talk to them about your future and ask them to help you walk through it. If you don't have a mentor, ask your parents, your trusted friends, or some wise people in your church to suggest someone who might be a good mentor for you.

READ:

Job 12:13, Psalm 111:10, Proverbs 3:13, and Acts 7:10

№16 THINKING ABOUT YOUR STRUGGLES

I have never been very good at studying or getting things done on time. In high school I was just smart enough to study for a small amount of time or put minimal work into projects and still get decent grades. I know I could have done better, but I was content to just get by without putting too much effort into anything. When I got to college this struggle with good study habits affected me. Because I didn't have good patterns and habits, my first year was a major struggle.

We all struggle with things, and while some situations are as simple as my story, others are major issues. You may have gotten caught up in a sin issue that you just can't seem to break free of, even though you want to change. There are so many different things that could have grabbed a hold of you, and you may really be having a difficult time getting past it. Now is a great time to work on these issues and learn tools to get past them before you graduate from high school. God likely has put people in your life and tools in front of you that will help—you just have to choose to use them.

THINK ABOUT:

1. Do you believe you have a good support base of people and tools to help you work on struggles and issues? If not, how can you find that support?

2. Are there issues in your life now that you want to break free of before you leave high school and your current support structures? How can other people help you with that?

3. What role does God play in freedom and recovery from issues?

THE WORLD THINKS:

Keep your issues hidden because if you bring them into the light, you will be judged. People aren't as loving and forgiving as they pretend to be.

ACT:

This one is tough. If you are dealing with any major issue or struggle, now is the time to work on breaking free. Pray and ask God to give you the right people in your life to help you. Find those people, and be honest with them. If you really want help and they are committed to you, they will help you. Ultimately, God is the one who provides freedom, but he often uses the people in our lives to encourage us and to open the doors to that freedom.

READ:

Ephesians 6:12, Colossians 1:29, and Hebrews 12:4

№ 17 STRENGTHENING YOUR FRIENDSHIPS

I recently ran into someone from high school at my new church. We weren't really close then, but it was someone that I had good memories of from my teen years. After I saw him, I went home that night and pulled out my yearbook from my senior year. I spent some time reading through what everyone had written, and a common theme emerged: people saying they wished we had gotten to know each other better and had been closer friends.

As I reflected upon those notes written so many years ago, I realized that I regret two things: First, I missed out on some really great friendships in high school because I wasn't willing to invest time with people; and second, I have let some friendships fade over the years that I should have maintained.

This year you have the opportunity to strengthen some of your close relationships and to even build upon some new ones. Seize that opportunity and build strong connections with classmates. Commit to specific ways you can stay in contact in the years ahead.

THINK ABOUT:

1. What are some ways you can strengthen friendships that you already have?

2. What people at school do you wish you had become friends with but hadn't—and why? What has stopped you from doing that?

3. Why do you think God has put the people in your life that he has? How do they help you grow closer to him?

THE WORLD THINKS:

You will probably never spend time with these people again and will likely forget them after high school, so don't waste too much time.

ACT:

Look for specific ways to strengthen some friendships. Start by honestly approaching your friends and simply talking with them about it. Being straightforward and saying you want a deeper friendship will go a long way toward encouraging growth. Another challenge is to think about people that you wish you were friends with but aren't. If that's a genuine desire, find a way to make it happen.

READ:

Exodus 33:11, Judges 11:37, Job 16:20-21, and Ecclesiastes 4:9-10

№18 THINKING ABOUT YOUR GIFTS AND TALENTS

God gave me the gift of teaching and preaching, but I didn't know it for a really long time. In fact, probably the only reason I discovered it was because of some people in my life who gave me opportunities to grow in those areas—they saw the beginning of those gifts in me.

As silly as it sounds, it all began when I was working at a summer camp and I was "game boy" leading all the crowdbreaker games and activities. My boss at the time affirmed that I had a good gift of having a healthy presence with a microphone in my hand and that I did a good job of leading hundreds of high school students from the front of the room.

The funny thing is that as I think back on that season of life, I wish I had the skills *then* that I have *now*. I believe I am exponentially better now than I was then. You may not really recognize the gifts and talents that God has given you, so be open to other people in your life who can help you see them. And then commit to developing those gifts and abilities in ways that honor God and serve the people in your life.

THINK ABOUT:

1. What are some of the gifts and talents you see in other people in your life?

2. How can you help your family and friends grow in their gifts and talents?

3. What are some of the gifts and talents you believe God has given you? How are you developing and using them?

THE WORLD THINKS:

The only gifts and talents that are truly worthwhile are the ones that can make you wealthy, powerful, or famous.

ACT:

Ask some people in your life if they can see the gifts and talents God has given you. Then ask them how you can best use those gifts to glorify God and to serve other people.

READ:

Proverbs 18:16, Ecclesiastes 5:19, Romans 6:23, 1 Corinthians 12:4, and James 1:17

NO.19 KEEPING DOORS OPEN

I've closed doors before that I don't think God wanted closed. I got out ahead of God with my own plans, and because I liked what I was doing, I shut things out that he might have used to lead me in his direction.

You have to make some big decisions your senior year, but you can do it in a way that allows God to lead and to change your plans if he wants. For example, if you are applying to colleges, consider applying to more than just the one school you want to attend because that wouldn't leave many open doors if that college says no. In the same way, hold loosely to your own plans because they may change—or God may change them.

I've already mentioned that my career plans were different from what God ultimately led me to do. If you had told me my senior year of high school that I would be a youth pastor for the majority of my life, I would have laughed at you. That was not in my plan at all, but God used summer camps, classrooms, internships, seminary, and ultimately someone losing their job (which opened the door for an interim job for me) to listen to him and take that step of faith. And it was a big, difficult, hard step, but God fully honored it, and time and time again he has affirmed it was right.

THINK ABOUT:

1. What door do you want to shut but haven't because God may be using it in your life?

2. How do you know when you are making the right decisions? Where does your affirmation come from?

3. Have you already shut some doors that you wish you could reopen? If so, what doors—and why do you want them reopened?

THE WORLD THINKS:

You need to do whatever you want and not worry about what anyone else thinks. Doors have to shut because there are just too many possibilities.

ACT:

Do some research on "life change" or "career change," and see if you can find some stories of people who made major life transitions. If you can't find anything, ask your parents or someone at your church to suggest someone to talk to. See why they changed directions and how they were able to walk away from what they had been doing.

READ:

Isaiah 45:1, Luke 13:24-25, Acts 5:19, and Revelation 3:8

NO.20 LEAVING A LEGACY

A lot of schools give seniors a chance to "leave a legacy" for younger students. In some cases it's a page in the yearbook where you dedicate things to others, and in other schools I've seen an entire wall where each senior has his or her own square to leave things. However it's done, this is a pretty neat practice.

All of us leave something behind. I mentioned before that my big place at school was within the band. So when I was leaving, I was literally handing over my place leading the band to a student who was coming up after me. This happens in sports, too, as we give away our roster spot to those who come after us. But we can also give less tangible things.

As a senior you have a place of influence and some power at your school. What if you took that influence and reached out to some younger students and gave them a place and a voice that they wouldn't normally have? How might you be able to change the lives of others by using the gifts and placement that you have as a senior? Oftentimes seniors just want to hold on to the power because they've finally gotten it after three years of high school—but what if your whole goal was to simply give it away and to bless other people with it? That would change things.

THINK ABOUT:

1. What is some of the legacy you will be leaving behind?

2. How might your legacy bless people and change their world?

3. Where is God in your legacy?

4. What could you do as a senior to give away power and control to younger students now?

THE WORLD THINKS:

No one did it for you, so why should you try to help out younger students now? Make them wait in line like you did. That's how it's always worked.

ACT:

Think about the students who were ahead of you at your school—maybe even decades ahead. What were some good legacies they left behind that have blessed you? Think about how you might be able to bless other younger students—both at school and at your youth group or church—and then do it.

READ:

Genesis 35:14-15, Joshua 4:7, and Psalm 118:22

SECTION 3

HEADING OUT THE DOOR

This is the most exciting point in the life of a senior. You have decided what you are going to do next year, and you're getting more and more excited for this next chapter in your life. Graduation is right around the corner, and it feels like you are finally at a place where the future is almost here. But at the same time you are excited to look back, and it's hard to believe that you have made it through the last 12 years of school—you are finally done with this stage of your life.

So as you get ready to head out the door, think about what things you want to take with you and how you want to be known in the next stage of life. Maybe you want to leave behind some habits and hang-ups that have been pulling you down. Maybe you want to change how people view you or work on modifying parts of your personality. You have the freedom to do and be almost anything in this next stage—that is both exciting and a little bit scary.

Your faith journey, too, will change. It is likely that you will have to find a new church. You won't be in a "youth group" anymore, and you may struggle to find the right fit for you. You will have to choose how you will live out your faith and what parts you want to focus on. So much excitement, change, and newness!

But guess what? You are ready.

№·21 DRAWING NEAR TO GOD

When I was in middle school, I remember a time when I was out in a rowboat near my house and it got really windy. I was trying to row my boat back to shore, but the wind was pushing me away. Still, I was making headway, even though it was really slow. I saw my dad standing on a beach really close to my house and I was rowing directly toward him. I almost made it, but one of my oars popped out of the oarlock and I lost all forward momentum.

The wind caught me sideways, and before I knew it I'd been pushed several hundred feet from the shore. I was too tired to try again, so I gave up. I was fortunate, though, because my dad saw me, so he drove the truck around to the place where I was going to end up and picked me up.

Sometimes our faith feels like that. We are doing everything we can to draw near to God but we're going against the wind and the current—and all of a sudden something pops up that takes us off course and throws us totally out of whack. Fortunately, like my dad was in that situation, God is faithful to pursue us; he doesn't just sit around waiting for us to get to him.

The one bit of advice I wish I could go back and give myself as a senior in high school would be to make sure that I established habits and patterns such as morning prayer, regular accountability with friends, more Bible reading, and connections to Christian adults because that would have helped me stay better connected to God.

THINK ABOUT:

1. What are some specific ways that draw you near to God?

2. What things in your life seem to push you away from God?

3. How can you ensure that you do more "drawing close" and less "pushing away" this year?

THE WORLD THINKS:

It's good enough to go to church on the weekend, if that's your thing, but you don't need to do anything else during the week. Religion is just one piece to your busy schedule; don't let it consume every part of your life.

ACT:

There are a lot of ways you can draw near to God. One idea: Spend a day in silence without a phone or connected device, and go to a place where you can pray, read Scripture, journal, and simply listen to God. If you don't know of a place, ask someone at your church to give you some suggestions.

READ:

Zephaniah 3:1-2, Hebrews 7:19, and Hebrews 10:19-22

№.22 CHOOSING YOUR PATH

Sometimes I make really bad decisions. I used to do a lot of rock climbing, and we loved to find places where people had gotten stuck and left behind expensive gear behind. We were pretty good climbers so we could generally get up to those points and "fleece" that gear off the rock. If you left something behind, then a better climber who could reach your stuff would get to keep it.

Unfortunately, I often thought I was a better climber than I was. So on plenty of occasions I would climb up to an abandoned piece of climbing equipment but get stuck there—unable to get it off the rock and return to the bottom. I was pretty good at picking a path up the rock, but I just wasn't very good at picking a path back down. I don't know how many times I got to the stuck spot and ended up having to use the same gear they had left behind, just to get myself down. That was always frustrating—especially when my friends would go up after me and recover the piece.

Picking the right path is never easy. But as a Christian, you have access to the Holy Spirit to lead you in the direction that God wants you to go. And the longer you follow God's path, the more clearly you'll recognize the signs, see the footprints of those who've gone before you, and get to the place you want to reach.

THINK ABOUT:

1. How do you know when you are on the path God has for you?

2. Have you ever gotten stuck jumping on a particular path in life and been unable to get back to your starting point? How did you deal with that situation?

3. Are you on any paths right now that you wish you weren't? How can other people help you to get back on the right one?

THE WORLD THINKS:

All roads of belief and faith lead to the same place and the same end result, so feel free to do whatever you want because you will eventually get to where you are supposed to be.

ACT:

We are often told that the right path in life is narrowly defined for us. But I'm not always convinced it is. For example, you probably face multiple choices for college and career—it isn't a narrow path at all. Sometimes we know...

READ:

Psalm 16:11, Proverbs 23:19, and Isaiah 40:14

№.23 ADJUSTING YOUR RELATIONSHIP WITH YOUR PARENTS

Everything changes when you leave home—whether that's for college, the military, or a career. Your relationship with your parents is one of the biggest changes. You won't have to check in with them before every decision or direction you go. They probably won't be asking about your homework or checking that you get enough sleep or seeing if you're eating well. No one will be doing your laundry, buying groceries, or making appointments for you. You will be in charge of so much more of your life.

For some people this is an incredibly scary thing, but for others it's clear that the time is right. A lot depends upon how your parents prepared you for this change or how much you anticipated it. When you return home on weekends or during holiday breaks, things are different, too. Going back into your home can cause tension and struggle. Honestly, the whole thing is a little bit weird. But it's a natural thing for everyone to go through.

On a positive note, it is easier to stay more connected than I could at your age. You can ask your parents questions via text, cell, or email. You can use technology to ask for help with the needs you still have, while at the same time creating space and boundaries.

THINK ABOUT:

1. How do you think this transition away from your parents will be for you? for them?

2. Do you believe you are ready for this change now? If not, how can you get ready?

3. What role do your parents have in your faith? Are you ready to really, truly own your faith for yourself? Why or why not?

THE WORLD THINKS:

It's time to break free of the bondage of your parents' rules. Now you can do whatever you want. Enjoy the freedom and take full advantage of it.

ACT:

Start writing a letter that you will give your parents or guardians when you leave. Put some significant time into it, thanking them for all they have done for you and listing what they have taught you and why it's significant. Share with them the legacy that they have built in you and the things that you will always take with you.

READ:

Proverbs 17:6, Luke 2:48, Colossians 3:20, and Hebrews 11:23

NO.24 TAKING YOUR FAITH TO COLLEGE

I went to a Christian college so it was fairly easy to take my faith with me. We had mandatory chapel and all kinds of opportunities to serve and stay close to God on campus. I went to church most Sundays, too, but never really got connected with a church or a college ministry.

If I could do it over again, I would have attended one church instead of going to a new one each year. I would have invested in it and allowed the church to invest in me. Fortunately, I received a lot of that investment at school, but when I graduated from college and left behind that Christian community, I didn't have the skills I needed in order to get connected to a local church again. It had been so right in front of me in college that I didn't have to look for it.

You may have a really solid faith, youth group, and church in high school and may already have plans to get connected in college. If that's the case then that is amazing. If you don't have that it will be much harder. What you are going to have to do is just decide to commit and make that a major priority in your life.

THINK ABOUT:

1. How important to you is it to take your faith to college, the military, or your career? What challenges to your faith do you expect to encounter?

2. Do you think being known as a Christian will limit the opportunities and fun you might have after high school? Why or why not?

3. What steps have you already thought about that will help you take your faith with you? What else could you do?

THE WORLD THINKS:

It's OK to take a break from your faith and come back to it when you have kids of your own. That's what everybody does.

ACT:

If your faith is important to you now, write a letter to yourself explaining why. Seal that letter up and ask your parents to mail it to you two months after you have gotten to college (or entered the military or moved to another community). Also, before you go, work with your home church to help you find a church where you are moving.

READ:

2 Chronicles 20:20, Matthew 6:30, 1 Corinthians 2:5, and Ephesians 2:8

№25 STARTING THE NEXT CHAPTER

Yes, you are about to start over. If you are heading to college, you will be a freshman again. Fortunately for you, it's a different kind of freshman. You aren't going back to what you were four years ago. The first year of college is a time of firsts again, but you likely won't encounter the same stigma attached to being new.

I believe a lot of people in college think about how much fun they had their first year and wish they could do it all over again. One cool thing is that you will have the freedom to decide if you want to be someone different. I don't mean faking a new personality; I just mean different.

I started college with the decision that I was going to be more outgoing and social. I had a head start because my sister was there before me, so I already knew some of her friends. But it was a big switch for me to decide that I was going to have fun and be in the middle of everything—totally different from my high school experience. And I had a great time.

You may have some things you want to leave behind in high school, or a struggle that you are walking away from. The first year after high school is a great time to do that. You won't carry any of your high school baggage, and you'll have a chance to make first impressions on a whole new crowd of people. What a great opportunity!

THINK ABOUT:

1. What are some things you are looking forward to during your first year after high school?

2. Do you want to make any changes to your personality or attempt things that are new or different? Why or why not?

3. How do you think your faith can better intersect with your life after high school?

THE WORLD THINKS:

You have the freedom to be who ever you want. Take advantage of that. Live life to the extreme, and don't have any regrets.

ACT:

As you are deciding what to do after high school, you also have the great freedom of choosing who you want to be. God has already given you a lot of gifts and tools to figure that out. Sit with a couple of close friends, and ask them how they see you and what things are holding you back from being that person.

READ:

Lamentations 3:23, Zephaniah 3:5, and Luke 5:37-38

NO.26 BUILDING NEW HABITS AND PATTERNS

You are hearing a lot in this section about things that will be new next year and how to leave stuff behind. The key to success after high school and to having your faith continue is creating new habits and patterns. Maybe you went to church on Sundays or youth group because your parents drove you or a friend picked you up. Maybe you regularly got a text or phone call from a small group leader. They helped your faith by keeping you accountable and in a pattern.

But those patterns likely will no longer exist when you leave. You will have to figure out new ones that work for you. Maybe for the first time you have the freedom to skip church on Sunday mornings because you found one that meets on Sunday nights, and that just feels better for you. Maybe you join a small group that meets at a different time during the week that fits your schedule better than the one you had in high school.

When you leave high school, be prepared to quickly establish healthy patterns for yourself or else it is almost inevitable that you will struggle. Most college and young adult pastors will say that if you don't establish solid faith patterns in your first three weeks of college, you will have a significantly harder time figuring that out. The same idea holds true if you're heading to the military or moving to a different place to begin your career. Wow, that's a scary thought—but it's a reminder of the power of healthy habits and patterns.

THINK ABOUT:

1. What are some faith patterns you want to establish that will work for you next year? How can you work on them now?

2. What habits do you currently have that you think are good ones? How can you take them with you?

3. What are some things you know will be a struggle? How can you put some strategies or habits in place now to help you handle them?

THE WORLD THINKS:

Do whatever you want—and if it doesn't work, just change it. You have the freedom to make all kinds of choices and live however you want.

ACT:

I hope you are starting to figure out what you are going to do next year. If you know where you might be, start doing research to find a church, ministry, or community of other Christ-followers that you can join. If possible, find a way to get there and meet people now. Anything you can do before you get there is a win.

READ:

Psalm 98:1, Isaiah 43:19, Mark 2:21, and Hebrews 10:24-25

№27 MAKING YOUR OWN DECISIONS

I still remember the first time I decided to skip class and sleep all day. I grew up in a pretty structured household, so this was a really big deal. It happened during my first quarter of college; I just decided I was tired and was going to stay in bed. It felt really good until I woke up around lunchtime and started to feel guilty.

Now, I knew I wasn't going to get in trouble. No one on my dorm floor was going to come and judge me. My parents weren't going to call and ask how class was that day. I was pretty convinced, too, that my professors wouldn't say anything. But deep down I knew that I had done something wrong, and I felt guilty about it. I had put expectations on myself that I would operate a certain way, and sleeping in and skipping things weren't part of who I wanted to be. It was one thing to sleep in on a Saturday. That was natural and expected—but to skip class that I was paying a lot of money for didn't feel right.

When you leave high school you have all kinds of freedoms that come your way really quickly. You will need to do a lot of self-reflection to consider what you will do in a variety of situations because it's often tough to make wise decisions in the middle of those moments.

THINK ABOUT:

1. How confident are you that you can make the right decisions?

2. When you make a wrong decision, how do you feel and respond?

3. Does making the wrong decisions push you away from God or draw you closer?

THE WORLD THINKS:

We all make mistakes. You will make a lot of them. But that's OK. Do it and move on.

ACT:

Take a sheet of paper and write down various scenarios that you might experience next year—tempting situations, opportunities for new experiences, times you feel overwhelmed or confused, and so on. Do a little bit of writing next to each potential scenario about how you want to respond. This simple preplanning can go a long way to helping you make good choices in the moment.

READ:

Isaiah 11:3, 2 Corinthians 9:7, and James 1:5

№ 28 DECIDING WHAT TO TAKE WITH YOU

During the days leading up to leaving home, you will probably do a lot of shopping. You'll buy things such as laundry baskets, shower totes, bedding, and other essential items. (Unless, of course, you're going into the military—and then you'll be selecting just a few things to take with you!) You will have to make your room a "home," and you'll need a bunch of those types of things to live.

But it's a little bit harder to decide what things to bring from your house or your room. It's not easy to simply pick a few things that will remind you of home, your family, and all your valued childhood and teenage memories—some photos and other things. But trying to encapsulate a life in a small box of trinkets is hard.

It's easier to think about bringing memories, values, and hopes. These things have been instilled in you for years, and they're an important part of who you are. When a new friend walks into your room, they'll look at the pictures and the knickknacks. But your memories, values, and hopes are your truly cherished items.

THINK ABOUT:

1. What are some of the values, memories, and stories you want to take with you to your new life?

2. What objects remind you of those highlights and are special to you? Which ones do you think you'll take with you once you leave home?

3. Do you have any objects that are significant to your faith journey that would give you opportunity to share with a new friend what you believe?

THE WORLD THINKS:

Don't take too much junk with you because you don't need it. You are going to make new friends and leave behind much of your past.

ACT:

With your youth group, small group, or just some Christian friends, brainstorm some tangible object (or objects) that you can take with you that will open the door to share your faith story with others.

READ:

Exodus 28:12, 1 Samuel 7:12, and 1 Thessalonians 3:6-8

NO.29 MAKING NEW FRIENDS

When I left for college, I went with five other people from my youth group. For the first couple of weeks of college, it was pretty easy to stay connected to them and not feel lonely. But I really wanted to meet new friends. I lived on a dorm floor with about 30 other guys, and we did a ton of things together. I made some really great friends that year and have amazing memories of that group.

Recently I've reconnected with some of them, and it's been really fun to talk through some of the things we did together—including some things that I had forgotten. So many of those memories involve us doing crazy things—like the night we decided to go hit golf balls into the ocean. We lived about four hours from the ocean, so this was a big commitment. But it was a great memory with friends who are still part of my life today.

Without a doubt I can say that I was shaped by my college friends. In particular, my faith was shaped and strengthened because many of them had such a solid faith. God put me exactly where I needed to be, around the people I needed to be with to help me grow. I pray that you have a similar experience with your friends after high school—people who will help your faith become deeper and stronger as you enter adulthood.

THINK ABOUT:

1. What do you value about your current friends? How can you best find those things in new friends?

2. How can you best maintain friendships with your old friends while at the same time making new ones?

3. Do you believe God can lead you to new friends? If so, how do you best think he can do that? If not, why not?

THE WORLD THINKS:

Most people don't have good friends. You're lucky if you have a couple in your lifetime. You shouldn't expect to make a lot of new ones after high school. Prepare to be alone.

ACT:

Before you finish high school, write out a list of what you value about your current friends. When you are heading off to your new life, keep this list close and look at it often for help, wisdom, and insight as you explore new friendships.

READ:

1 John 4:11 and 3 John 1:2

^{NO.}30 SAYING GOODBYE

It's never easy to say goodbye. I remember the moment my parents dropped me off at college and were walking out the door. After they left, I shut the door, sat on my bed, and just thought about what had happened. I loved them a ton and they were such a strong support base for me, but everything was about to be different. It was hugely emotional, and I had to take a few minutes to sit there and just think about it.

You may have already dealt with a number of goodbyes in your life. Perhaps you moved at some point and had to say goodbye to some special friends. Or maybe you experienced a death in your family and faced the emotional experience of loss. We all deal with goodbyes in different ways. Some of us just want to get them over with as soon as possible; we can't wait for it to end. The opposite is true for other people, who draw it out as long as possible.

One thing that's true with any goodbye, no matter what, is some sort of loss. When you leave home you are saying goodbye to family, friends, routines, patterns, safety, and security. You are embarking on a new journey where you will have to figure out all of those things on your own. Scary stuff, but this is exactly what you have been preparing for. This is where the adventure truly begins.

THINK ABOUT:

1. What do you think is going to be the most difficult goodbye? Why?

2. How much loss and change have you experienced in your life? How have those experiences affected you?

3. Do you have a firm foundation to know how to best look for healthy ways of filling the void after the goodbyes? If not, how can you build that foundation?

THE WORLD THINKS:

Just get over it and move on. Everyone deals with pain and loss.

ACT:

Write some goodbye notes—real ones with paper and pens, not electronic ones with text messages and social media. Tell people how much you will miss them and what their relationship means to you. Prepare them for the loss—you aren't the only one experiencing it.

READ:

Ecclesiastes 3:1-15, John 3:16, and 2 Corinthians 13:11

FOLLOW-UP

So there you have it. You're a senior and soon you will head off into the wild blue yonder. You've spent a lot of time preparing for the future, and it is almost upon you. Where will you go? What will you do? How will you make decisions? Where does your faith play out in all of this?

You've prepared for the future—now it's time to see what the future holds. Even if you are staying home and working or going to a local college, there will be change and loss—and if you head off to college or enter the military, you'll experience major change and loss!

I hope that these devotions have caused you to think and that the actions steps and Bible verses have helped you build a healthy foundation. You can do this, and God is so proud of you and who you are becoming. Remember that you are his workmanship and he builds beautiful things!